GREAT ESCAPES

THE LOST BOYS OF SUDAN

Jeff Burlingame

CAUTION !
16,000
CHILDREN
AHEAD

Marshall Cavendish
Benchmark
New York

"Thanks to Lauren Foster, Dr. Richard Lobban, and Dave Wilkins for their assistance with this book."

Other Marshall Cavendish Offices:
Marshall Cavendish International (Asia) Private Limited, 1 New Industrial Road, Singapore 536196 • Marshall Cavendish International (Thailand) Co Ltd. 253 Asoke, 12th Flr, Sukhumvit 21 Road, Klongtoey Nua, Wattana, Bangkok 10110, Thailand • Marshall Cavendish (Malaysia) Sdn Bhd, Times Subang, Lot 46, Subang Hi-Tech Industrial Park, Batu Tiga, 40000 Shah Alam, Selangor Darul Ehsan, Malaysia

Marshall Cavendish is a trademark of Times Publishing Limited
All websites were available and accurate when this book was sent to press.

Library of Congress Cataloging-in-Publication Data
Burlingame, Jeff.
The Lost Boys of Sudan / Jeff Burlingame.
p. cm. — (Great escapes)
Summary: "Presents accounts of narrow escapes executed by oppressed individuals and groups while illuminating social issues and the historical background that led to wars in Sudan and the orphaned refugees known as the 'Lost Boys'"—Provided by publisher.
Includes bibliographical references and index.
ISBN-13: 978-1-60870-475-0 (print)
ISBN-13: 978-1-60870-696-6 (ebook)
1. Children and war—Sudan--Juvenile literature. 2. War victims—Sudan—Juvenile literature. 3. Refugees—Sudan—Juvenile literature. 4. Sudan—History—Juvenile literature. I. Title. II. Series: Great escapes (Marshall Cavendish Benchmark)

HV640.5.S9B86 2011
962.404'3--dc22
2011005596

Senior Editor: Deborah Grahame-Smith
Publisher: Michelle Bisson
Art Director: Anahid Hamparian
Series Designer: Kay Petronio

Photo research by Linda Sykes
The photographs in this book are used by permission and through the courtesy of: Howard Davies/Corbis: Cover; Scott Peterson/Getty Images: 4; De Agnostini/Getty Images: 11; Jerry Gray/AP Images: 14; Randy Olson/National Geographic Image Collection/Getty Images: 20; Sipa via AP Images: 25; Chris Rainier/Corbis: 27; Jim Cooper/AP Images: 29; Chris Rainier/Corbis: 32; Wendy Stone/Sygma/Corbis: 34; Brennan Linsley/AP Images: 37; Scott Peterson/Getty Images: 39; Bernard Bisson/Sygma/Corbis: 42; Nasser Nasser/AP Images: 45; AFP/Getty Images: 48; Dave Kolpack/AP Images: 50; Al Goldis/AP Photo: 52; ©Newmarket/National Geographic Films: 54; Salt Lake Tribune, Scott Sommerdorf/AP Images: 57; John Bohn/AP Images: 66; Courtesy Dept. of Labor/AP Images: 67.

Printed in Malaysia (T)
135642

GREAT ESCAPES

THE LOST BOYS OF SUDAN

Jeff Burlingame

CAUTION !
16,000
CHILDREN
AHEAD

Marshall Cavendish
Benchmark
New York

"Thanks to Lauren Foster, Dr. Richard Lobban, and Dave Wilkins for their assistance with this book."

Other Marshall Cavendish Offices:
Marshall Cavendish International (Asia) Private Limited, 1 New Industrial Road, Singapore 536196 • Marshall Cavendish International (Thailand) Co Ltd. 253 Asoke, 12th Flr, Sukhumvit 21 Road, Klongtoey Nua, Wattana, Bangkok 10110, Thailand • Marshall Cavendish (Malaysia) Sdn Bhd, Times Subang, Lot 46, Subang Hi-Tech Industrial Park, Batu Tiga, 40000 Shah Alam, Selangor Darul Ehsan, Malaysia

Marshall Cavendish is a trademark of Times Publishing Limited
All websites were available and accurate when this book was sent to press.

Library of Congress Cataloging-in-Publication Data
Burlingame, Jeff.
The Lost Boys of Sudan / Jeff Burlingame.
p. cm. — (Great escapes)
Summary: "Presents accounts of narrow escapes executed by oppressed individuals and groups while illuminating social issues and the historical background that led to wars in Sudan and the orphaned refugees known as the 'Lost Boys'"—Provided by publisher.
Includes bibliographical references and index.
ISBN-13: 978-1-60870-475-0 (print)
ISBN-13: 978-1-60870-696-6 (ebook)
1. Children and war—Sudan—Juvenile literature. 2. War victims—Sudan—Juvenile literature. 3. Refugees—Sudan—Juvenile literature. 4. Sudan—History—Juvenile literature. I. Title. II. Series: Great escapes (Marshall Cavendish Benchmark)

HV640.5.S9B86 2011
962.404'3--dc22
2011005596

Senior Editor: Deborah Grahame-Smith
Publisher: Michelle Bisson
Art Director: Anahid Hamparian
Series Designer: Kay Petronio

Photo research by Linda Sykes
The photographs in this book are used by permission and through the courtesy of: Howard Davies/Corbis: Cover; Scott Peterson/Getty Images: 4; De Agnostini/Getty Images: 11; Jerry Gray/AP Images: 14; Randy Olson/National Geographic Image Collection/Getty Images: 20; Sipa via AP Images: 25; Chris Rainier/Corbis: 27; Jim Cooper/AP Images: 29; Chris Rainier/ Corbis: 32; Wendy Stone/Sygma/Corbis: 34; Brennan Linsley/AP Images: 37; Scott Peterson/ Getty Images: 39; Bernard Bisson/Sygma/Corbis: 42; Nasser Nasser/AP Images: 45; AFP/ Getty Images: 48; Dave Kolpack/AP Images: 50; Al Goldis/AP Photo: 52; ©Newmarket/ National Geographic Films: 54; Salt Lake Tribune, Scott Sommerdorf/AP Images: 57; John Bohn/AP Images: 66; Courtesy Dept. of Labor/AP Images: 67.

Printed in Malaysia (T)
135642

CONTENTS

A group of Sudanese Lost Boys gathers at a Kenyan refugee camp in 1992, the same year David Bol was shot by militants as he slept.

INTRODUCTION

"I JUST WISHED
I WAS DEAD"

David Bol was asleep the moment his life changed forever.

"It sounded like a dream," he said. "I could see the bullets flying and making noise—it *was* like a dream. I didn't even feel pain. And then I tried to get up so I could run. . . . "

Running should have been easy for the thirteen-year-old boy. For nearly half his life he had been running barefoot across southern Sudan's scorching soil and swampy grasslands. He was searching for refuge from both his own government and the rogue militants bent on destroying the villages of his people and killing families in the name of a complex civil war. Running was one thing Bol knew. Yet on this occasion—in the middle of the night on another nameless day in 1992—he could no longer run.

"I was so heavy I couldn't get up at all," he said. "I was like, 'What is going on?' I put my elbow down and tried to get myself up while they were still shooting." Bol could not muster the strength. "So I got back down," he said, "and then I could feel the blood, like something wet." He soon realized what had happened. He had been shot in the back.

Bol had been ambushed—randomly attacked—as he slept under the cool desert sky. The militants he had been running from for years finally had caught up with him, and they had done permanent damage.

The first sounds of gunfire had scattered Bol's fellow refugees across the land. Now, no one was left to help the feeble boy. He could only rely on his instincts, and they told him to flip onto his side. Get the wound up in the air. Slow the bleeding. In front of him lay another boy who also had been shot. "He was yelling," Bol said. "He was dying, you know. He died right away."

When the militants left, the refugees who had fled upon their arrival returned to camp. Someone carried Bol to a nearby site that had been set up for the injured. The air was filled with screams of pain from other refugees. Some had been shot; others had been trampled because they had not woken up quickly enough. There was neither medicine nor a doctor, so Bol's injury was treated crudely. Someone wrapped his clothes around the wound to stop the bleeding. "It was so painful," he said. "Memories were flying in my head. I just wished I was dead. I wished I would die so I wouldn't have to deal with the pain."

The next day, Bol was loaded into a truck with the other injured refugees and driven to a hospital in a nearby town. But the small hospital was not equipped to deal with his extensive injuries. The bullet had ripped a large chunk of flesh from his back, had severed his intestines, and had broken several bones. So, again, health workers loaded him into a truck—placing him on a mattress in the back alongside others who were injured— and drove him across jarring roads to a larger hospital in Kenya. Surgeons operated on him and gave him several skin grafts, and Bol spent the next six months recovering.

Given his experiences, it is difficult to call Bol one of the lucky ones. But in many respects, he was. Nine years after he was shot, Bol became one of 3,800 southern Sudanese refugees selected to move to the United States as part of a massive resettlement program. Most of those 3,800 had been orphans and had seen their villages burned in government-sponsored attacks. They had seen their family members suffer violent deaths and had watched their peers waste away to near skeletons from starvation and then collapse beside the road to die. They had survived thousand-mile treks across the countryside, avoided wild animals, and battled diseases. Their numbers had reduced from nearly 30,000 to just 11,000. Someone had given these refugees a name: the Lost Boys.

"I'm not sure I was lost," Bol said. "It was almost like I was walking in the dark and you don't know where you were going."

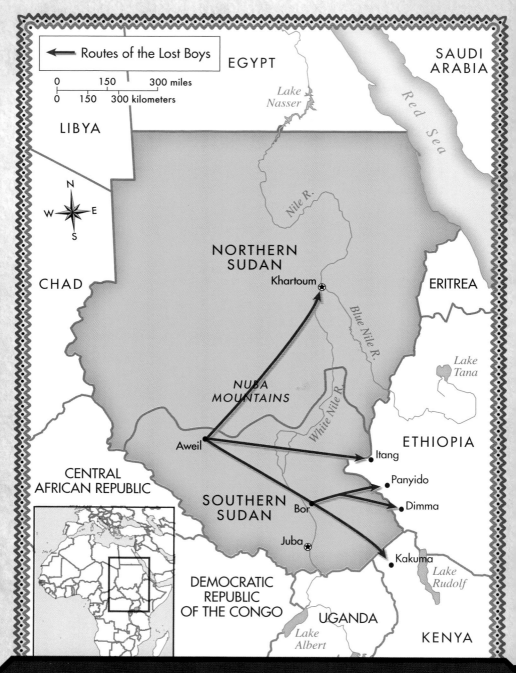

By 1989, millions of southern Sudanese had been forced to leave their homes. Some fled to the northern city of Khartoum. Others, countless Lost Boys, left their villages near the cities of Aweil and Bor for refugee camps such as Itang, Panyido, and Dimma in Ethiopia, and Kakuma in Kenya.

SUDAN'S TROUBLED HISTORY

For centuries, world maps showed Sudan as just one African country. Beginning in 2011, it officially became two—North Sudan and South Sudan. But for those who live there, the country has long been known to be at least two distinct regions. There is northern Sudan, a desert-dominated region primarily populated by Arab Muslims. Then there is southern Sudan, which has a hot and humid equatorial climate. Its population is made up of Nilotes, a generic term used to describe many of the region's ethnic groups, who speak a variety of Nilotic languages. The largest of the southern Sudanese ethnic groups is the Dinka. In southern Sudan, people practice a variety of native religions, although there also are many Christians who were converted by missionaries.

For much of the past fifty-five years, Sudan's northern and southern regions have been fighting each other in deadly wars that have killed millions of people and displaced many millions more. Among those displaced—and also among those who were killed—was the group of orphaned refugees now known as the Lost Boys.

Though violence and war mar its recent past, Sudan's lengthy history has included periods of peace. The lifeline of this northeast African country is the roughly 4,100-mile-long (6,600-kilometer-long) Nile River, whose waters flow north from equatorial Africa through the swampy Sudd region to the Sahara Desert and into the Mediterranean Sea. Civilizations throughout history have used the revered Nile for sustenance and transport. The river's fertile banks offer quality land for growing crops, and its waters give the area's inhabitants a means of transportation and sustenance. Today, the Nile travels through nine countries, including Sudan, which it splits in two geographic regions, east and west. Mountains, including the Nuba range, separate Sudan's arid north from its geographically diverse south.

Some historians estimate that human ancestors lived in the area of modern-day Sudan 5 million years ago. Archaeologists have found artifacts from human civilizations dating to the middle of the Mesolithic era—roughly 8000 BCE. During that era, settlers lived in hamlets made of mud and bricks. For sustenance they fished and hunted along the Nile, grew grain, and raised cattle.

Around 1570 BCE, Kush became part of the Egyptian New Kingdom. It remained part of Egypt for the next five hundred years, until the Egyptian dynasty crumbled and Kush became an independent kingdom again. Today, temples dedicated to Egyptian and Nubian gods still stand in Sudan. Portions of the Kush kingdom lasted until about the first century CE.

Christianity arrived in Sudan around 540 CE, when Byzantine empress Theodora sent a missionary to preach the gospel of Jesus Christ to the Nubians who were living there. Christian kingdoms reigned over the Nile valley for a thousand years, but eventually Arab Muslims took over. In 1898, a joint British-Egyptian army conquered Sudan. In theory, the two countries were to rule Sudan together, but in practice Sudan essentially became a British colony. In northern Sudan, especially in the fertile areas along the Nile River, the British introduced new technologies that helped to industrialize and develop the region. Meanwhile, they all but ignored southern Sudan. In fact, because they believed that this tribe-dominated area was incapable of handling such innovations, British leaders closed southern Sudan to all outsiders. Northern Sudanese were banned from living or working in the south.

In the 1920s and 1930s, new waves of nationalism sprang up in Sudan. The goal of the movement was to unify the north and the south. This eventually happened in January 1956, when Sudan officially became an independent republic. The British and Egyptian troops that had long occupied the country withdrew. Sudan's direct association with Egypt ended once again.

This illustration depicts southern Sudanese tribesmen battling British forces in 1884 during what was known as the Battle of Tamanieb.

WHAT'S IN A NAME?

Throughout the years, many people have been confused about exactly where the word *Sudan* comes from. It is derived from an Arabic phrase *Bilad al-Sudan*, which translates to "Land of the Blacks." Scholars have proposed different theories about the country's name. One theory is that the word comes from the term *sudd*, which is a large, swampy area. Indeed, the White Nile River forms such an area in southern Sudan.

Sudan's newfound independence united the country in name only. The northern and southern regions still did not see eye to eye. In fact, just five months prior to the official date of independence, a group of southern soldiers staged a mutiny in the city of Torit. They refused to follow an order transferring them to posts under the command of northern officers. Several hundred northerners, including merchants, government officials, and military officers, were killed during the mutiny. The government quickly gained control of the situation and executed seventy southerners for their roles in the mutiny. The executions had nowhere near the impact of the initial mutiny, however.

Southerners remained unhappy about the lack of power they were granted under the new government and fearful of being controlled by the Arab Muslims of the north. They continued to rebel. The Torit incident helped lead to the creation of the Anya-Nya, a group of separatist guerrillas in the south. The group included some of the original mutineers who had escaped punishment, as well as many other younger southern students.

The mutiny, along with the creation of the Anya-Nya, marked the beginning of Sudan's first civil war. In a pamphlet he wrote years later, Anya-Nya leader Joseph Lagu stated why his group had decided to wage war against the north:

> As the British started leaving the South, their administrative posts and business firms were taken up by Northern Sudanese who previously had not been allowed to work or settle in the South. The Southerners began to feel more and more strongly that their country was being colonized by Arabs and that their great expectations from independence boiled down to the replacement of one master by another. The Northern officials looked down upon the Southerners, openly discriminating against them and on the whole treated them as subject people. . . . They kept on insulting and abusing us, often using the word *abeed* [slaves] when referring to Southerners. Only one thing stood out clearly and this was what the Arabs themselves wanted then . . . : to dominate and colonize the South. To achieve this they try to impose on us Africans their religion, language and customs. By this method they want to turn us into Arabs and thereby conquer our country for good.

At first poorly armed and incapable of doing major damage, the Anya-Nya soon gained the support of other countries, including Germany, Uganda, and Israel, which trained Anya-Nya soldiers and sold them weapons. Still, the relatively small Anya-Nya organization proved to be no match for Sudan's government troops. Anya-Nya's soldiers based themselves in the rural southern countryside and in Uganda, while Sudanese troops occupied the major towns.

The unrest continued throughout Sudan for years. In May 1969, a group of young army officers led by Jafaar Nimeiri staged a coup and seized control of the Sudanese government. This act ended years of civilian control, which had been fraught with economic problems. The following month, the new regime issued a declaration that granted autonomy to the south. Southerner Joseph Garang led the new Ministry of Southern Affairs. Garang's reign did not last long, however. In 1971, he was implicated as part of a communist coup and hanged.

Meanwhile, in 1971, Joseph Lagu created a form of government called the Southern Sudan Liberation Movement (SSLM). The following year, leaders from the SSLM and the federal government met in Addis Ababa, Ethiopia, to discuss an end to the civil war. That end came in early 1972, when the two sides signed a peace pact that granted the south a high

John Garang (not to be confused with Joseph Garang), leader of the Sudan People's Liberation Army, is seen here on September 11, 1986, near the town of Kapoeta in southeastern Sudan.

degree of autonomy. As historians J. Millard Burr and Robert O. Collins note in their book *Requiem for the Sudan,*

> The agreement halted a conflict that for over seventeen years had devastated the South and caused the deaths of an estimated half million southerners. The region's population had been scattered like chaff in the wind; some two hundred thousand Sudanese were found in neighboring countries and five hundred thousand of those displaced had burrowed into the hinterland, or bush, of Southern Sudan.

Southern Sudan finally had achieved some semblance of equality. Or so its people hoped.

A Second Civil War

Technically, the following eleven years were peaceful, although the south continued to suffer exploitation and discrimination at the hands of the north. Most of Sudan's new economic development was still occurring in the north. Even when people discovered oil in the south, northern politicians redefined the country's boundaries so that the moneymaking, oil-producing regions would be part of the north.

The fragile period of peace was shattered in September 1983, when Nimeiri—who, ironically, had signed the Addis Ababa peace accord some twelve years earlier—declared that Islamic law would govern all of Sudan. The law called for harsh punishments such as amputation, execution, and flogging. This declaration angered southerners, most of whom were not Muslims. It was the final straw for the southern-based Sudan People's Liberation Movement (SPLM), whose military branch, the Sudan People's Liberation Army (SPLA), began fighting for many of the same objectives the south had battled for during the first civil war. Eventually joining the SPLA were members of the new Anya-Nya, or Anya-Nya II, which had re-formed a few years earlier, as well as many members of the

Dinka and Nuer ethnic groups. The second Sudanese civil war was under way.

As was the case during the first civil war, the southern soldiers initially were poorly armed and did not present much of a challenge to those from the better-equipped north. Again, however, other countries began to supply the southern soldiers with arms. This time Libya and Ethiopia were major contributors, offering the SPLA guns and missiles powerful enough to shoot down northern aircraft as they flew overhead.

Because the SPLA's leader, John Garang, was a Dinka, the Dinkas' homes and villages became the primary target of many of the most brutal attacks from the north. Soldiers destroyed the Dinkas' crops, raped Dinka women, took their children as slaves, and killed both men and cattle.

David Bol remembers exactly what life was like as he was growing up in his Dinka village. He was just four years old when the war began, and he spent the next four years living in fear of what it might mean to him and his family. He said,

> You grow up witnessing all this stuff and most of us probably witnessed different things in different places. Maybe the government would come up [and] you see homes being burned and people running every day up to the forest to hide when you hear the bangs or gunshots coming over the village. It was almost like a daily thing, you know. . . . seeing people killed or hearing guns every day. It was a difficult time growing up. You get to see what the war is all about—people being killed and people dying and being kicked out of your own house or your own village and things being burned down. There wasn't anything else that we knew. It was just hide or run away or die. You had to be on your feet all the time and try to stay alive. At that young age we didn't know what war is or what the fighting is all about, we just had to go with the flow, when people run, you run.

SUDAN'S DINKA PEOPLE

In geographic areas where different environments meet, there often are cultural clashes as well. Such has been the history of Sudan's Dinka people. The Dinka are the largest ethnic group in southern Sudan. Outside powers, from the ancient Egyptians to the Ottoman Empire and the British, have repeatedly invaded and colonized Sudan over the centuries. Sudan became a place where world powers drew the border between Islam and the older religions of Africa. Unfortunately for the Dinka, this left them as a non-Muslim minority in a nation whose government is led by a Muslim majority with little interest in their welfare.

Cultural differences have extended to government structures as well. Whereas northern Sudanese are more modernized, the Dinka are a traditional people. And while poverty is widespread in Sudan, the Dinka, who live as farmers and cattle herders, are particularly poor by Western standards.

Dinka tribes are organized at the village level. Men occupy the leadership positions, and each village traces its ancestry through the male leaders. Women generally perform household and farming tasks while young men herd cattle. Because of cultural differences, most Dinka have viewed Sudan's civil wars as invasions from the north rather than internal conflicts. The tribe's reliance on village-by-village governance, along with its widespread poverty, has hampered the organization of antigovernment insurgent groups among the Dinka. More than 1 million Dinka, Nuer, and Equatorians have been killed during the country's internal upheavals. Many more have fled to nearby countries such as Kenya and Uganda, which have large populations of Dinka refugees.

Bol eventually did a lot of running. "You had no other options," he said. "Your cattle had been taken away. You had nothing to eat. We just had to get away."

Millions of southern Sudanese had to get away. They were forced to leave their homes, either to escape the fighting or simply to avoid starving to death after soldiers took their cattle or destroyed their crops. By 1989, some 1 million southerners had fled to Sudan's capital, the northern city of Khartoum.

DINKA SURNAMES

In most cultures, surnames—also known as family names or last names—have meanings associated with them and are passed down from generation to generation. Initially, people used surnames to help distinguish among individuals who had the same first, or given, name. Surnames were often derived from a person's occupation, place of residence, or other personal details. Here is a list of some of the Dinka surnames found in this book and their meanings. Note that the meanings of many names fluctuate, based on variations in dialect and interpretation.

Achak: ingenious or creative person
Alek: leader in fighting or hunting
Anyieth: sweet sugar cane
Awino: good luck
Bior: white (teeth)
Dau: young female heifer
Deng: ancestor, god

Gam: believe
Garang: ancestor of mankind; Adam
Jal: visitor or guest
Majok: black bull with white chest
Ngong: poor, unhappy
Wek: parade with a bull

About 350,000 southerners had wound up in the neighboring country of Ethiopia, and many hundreds of thousands were scattered elsewhere across the region.

John Bul Dau, also a Dinka, was a young boy when he began to hear rumblings of what the war might mean to him one day. First, his parents told him a story about a man who met a tortoise one day while he was out for a walk. The tortoise told the man, "I am sent by the Lord. I bring you news of doom. Your country, southern Sudan, will be destroyed." The tortoise then gave the man three options. He could choose the way his village would be destroyed: drought, flood, or war. The man chose war. People retold this tale, and other similar ones, throughout Dau's village. His people began to debate what they would do if the choice of drought, flood, or war came to them. They also debated what they would do in each instance. Dau said, "War would come to us, but God would be with us in our hour of torment and make us powerful again. This was the secret strength of the southern Sudanese. We would never give up, despite being outnumbered and outgunned because we knew we would triumph in the end."

As Dau grew older, war moved closer. "Each night I tried to force some milk past my tongue," he said, "but the sound of bombs exploding somewhere in the distance beyond my village made my stomach hurt and my throat clamp shut, like the jaw of a crocodile. I went to bed with my stomach growling and my head roiling with thoughts of what might come."

It was not long before Dau discovered firsthand what the war was all about.

A Dinka man leads his cattle into the trees near Khawr Biem Rom, southern Sudan, in an effort to escape government forces.

BECOMING LOST BOYS

David Bol was eight years old when the soldiers attacked his village in 1987. It happened in the middle of the night when he and his family—minus his father, who, like many Dinka men, was off fighting in the war—were asleep. Bol said,

> What the militia would do or the government would do is just come at night when everyone was asleep because they know that is the only time they could find people. When they come, they expect people will be at home, you know? So they usually come at night and if you're not lucky enough and you're the first village that they get to you don't have time to escape, but if you're far away a little bit then you can hear maybe the gunfire, the tank roaring and then gunshots and all this stuff that will give you time to run in the middle of the night.

In Bol's case, there was no warning. Instead, gunfire seemed to erupt from out of nowhere. The entire village left their homes and scrambled at the first frightening sounds. To avoid being shot, captured, or taken hostage, Bol fled in a random direction. The rest of his family—his mother, his brother, and three sisters—went another way. Bol never saw them again.

"It's really tough, you know, tough to be thrown out of a village or a house or what you call a home for most of your life," Bol said. But he had to leave. His other choice was to stay, which really was not an option because the soldiers were torching homes whether people were in them or not. Bol ran until he reached the next village, where he joined another group that was fleeing. Together, they ran to the next village and joined others. The displaced Dinka repeated this pattern as they searched for refuge from the war that finally had arrived in their land.

Other Lost Boys faced similar situations when they were forced to flee their homes. Daniel Khoch, for example, was six or seven years old—exact ages for many Lost Boys have never been determined—when soldiers attacked his village in southwestern Sudan. For him, the attack was a two-day-long nightmare. The first day was a Sunday, and Khoch was playing soccer after the end of a service at his Catholic church. Out of the blue, he heard the sound of a "plane they use to bomb the people" and began to run. Everyone around him ran. His mother and his brother went in a different direction, and Khoch did not hear anything about their whereabouts for the next fifteen years.

Later that day, Khoch returned home and found his father and his sister. Khoch spent the next day tending to cattle in the fields and worrying about his mother and brother. When the day's work was done, he returned home to find men using rifles to shoot people. In an English assignment he wrote years later, Khoch described exactly what he saw that day:

> It came a strange sound and screaming of
> people of which I didn't heard [sic] one day in
> my live [sic]. Within zero minutes, the sound
> and screaming of people getting louder and
> louder, immediately, I saw many people running
> dizzinessly [sic] in different directions
> without control at all. . . . As sooner as they
> pass by near me, one of the people who were
> been running, called out to me with unwanted
> voice saying, "Please, please, come on. Let us
> go together. Here are Arabs soldiers. They will
> kill you if you don't run."

Khoch did not get killed. He ran.

John Chol Kon was only five years old when he fled his village. The military attacked while he was staying at a friend's house. He recalled,

> We heard sounds of so many bullets and
> immediately realized that there was serious
> fighting. We were very terrified and began
> crying with much fear. My friend's parents
> took us out, and we began running in a very
> confused way. In the process, I lost my friend
> and his parents and found myself in the
> company of another family, who allowed me to
> join them. . . . I haven't seen my parents again. I
> don't know why my village was attacked, but
> I have heard that the government of Sudan,
> which is very strong, has been fighting with
> our leader. They have killed many of our people.

Although it would be years before they were labeled as such, David Bol, Daniel Khoch, and John Chol Kon became Lost Boys on the days they fled their homes without their parents. The Lost Boys were the group of roughly 30,000 southern Sudanese children—mostly Dinka and Nuer boys of ages four to seventeen—who left their homes and families during their country's second civil war to find refuge in northern Sudanese cities, foreign countries, and other places.

The Lost Boys' name came from international aid workers, who likened the children's situation to that of the orphans in J. M. Barrie's children's book, *Peter Pan*. In Barrie's fictional story, a group of orphans called the Lost Boys joins with a character named Peter Pan in order to survive in an adult-dominated world. This is similar to what Sudan's Lost Boys were forced to do. But their struggle to survive was not fictional.

Some of Sudan's real-life Lost Boys were unhappy with the label—that is, once they learned about it. Most never heard the term until many years later, when they reached the United States. "The connotation in the U.S. implied that we were lost and that we didn't know anything, that we had no nation, no families, that we were unruly," said Valentino Achak Deng, who fled his village in southern Sudan when he was nine years old. "But I never considered myself lost, not a single day, even when I would see a fellow countryman dead, I knew that I was doing something that would be tangible in the future, if I was to survive." Another Lost Boy, quoted anonymously in a study done in 1992, said, "My country is not the first country to go to war. There is war in the world. The title [Lost Boys] is not good. We are not ignorant. Lost things are not good because they are useless. I preferred being called an unaccompanied minor, because that is what we were. They can call us 'Boys of Sudan!'"

Other Lost Boys have found the term tolerable, and some have even enjoyed it. David Bol said, "I don't have a problem with it at all. You really don't know where you were going. You didn't have anybody that's taking care of you. If you put all of that together, it's like, 'Lost Boys.' But it's different depending on how people look at it."

Deng Malou, a Sudanese refugee who eventually found a home in Boston, Massachusetts, said he takes no offense when someone calls him a Lost Boy. His circle of fellow refugees does not seem to mind the term, either. Malou said, "We like it, it's a

Valentino Achak Deng fled his village when he was nine years old. He is pictured here in 2008 in New York City at an event held to honor philanthropists.

title, our survivor name. It's a good name for us, even now that we are men we don't mind."

Experts in Sudanese culture agree that the nickname Lost Boys has both good and bad characteristics. One of these experts is Dr. Dianna Shandy, director of African studies at Macalester College in St. Paul, Minnesota, and author of the book *Nuer-American Passages: Globalizing Sudanese Migration*. "That label is both a benefit and a detriment, depending on the situation or the context," she said. A benefit is that the name helps generate compassion, and people "can associate that with a very traumatic and terrible set of

WHAT ABOUT THE LOST GIRLS?

People have written books and directed several movies about the Lost Boys of Sudan, but little has been written about Sudan's Lost Girls. Although most people have never heard of them, there actually were female refugees. However, of the 3,800 orphaned refugees who were relocated to the United States, fewer than 100 were female.

One of the reasons for this was that it was difficult to identify exactly who the Lost Girls were. When girls arrived at refugee camps, such as the one in Kakuma, Kenya, people immediately placed them with foster families because they considered girls more vulnerable than boys. This allowed the girls to sort of "disappear" from the crowds of refugees. Believing they had done their jobs and had taken care of the girls, aid workers focused more attention on caring for the boys. When it came time to determine who the original "lost children" were, it was far easier to identify the boys. Complicating matters was the fact that the foster families that took in the girls were poor, and they knew they could receive money or goods from whatever man eventually married their new "daughter." For this and other reasons, many families became reluctant to disclose the girls' whereabouts.

Ayen, an eighteen-year-old girl living at the refugee camp in Kakuma, discussed this issue with a journalist in 2002. She said, "The problem is that my foster-parents could find a rich man, and then they will marry me off. Even if I don't want to go [with the man], they will insist."

The fact that many foster families used Lost Girls as servants also worked against their chances of traveling to America. The families did not want to give up their source of free labor. Lost Girl Grace Anyieth was seventeen years old in 2002, when she told a reporter what her daily chores were. They included cooking, cleaning, washing, walking to get water, and babysitting. She wondered why the boys had the chance to come to America, but not the girls. "Why not the girls?" she said. "I would have liked the chance to go abroad. You can be free there. Free to work, free to study."

Bad timing was another reason for the low number of Lost Girls. Since girls generally were at home when militants raided their villages, the girls often were taken captive before they could flee. The boys, on the other hand, frequently were working in the fields when their villages were attacked. This meant they usually joined the groups of other, mostly male, refugees on their trek across the desert.

These two girls are shown at their refugee camp in Kassala, Sudan, during the famine of 1984–1985.

circumstances." On the negative side, Shandy said, "I think there is an issue with refugees if you emphasize the negative or the lack of or the gap of what's not there, as opposed to emphasizing the agency or the positive attributes. So by calling these folks 'Lost Boys' it's focusing on what they don't have or didn't have as opposed to what they may well have accomplished or what they aspire to accomplish."

Most of the Lost Boys of Sudan were either Dinka or Nuer—two traditional peoples with a storied history of battling each other over cattle and land. Yet during the second civil war, members of both groups had been forced to unite as refugees escaping government-backed militias intent on doing as much damage as possible to southerners. One such militia was known as the *murahalin*, or *murahaleen*, which is Arabic for "wanderer." Murahalin raids on southern Sudanese tribes were infamous for their brutality. The murahalin's typical methods of attack included abducting women and children and forcing them into slavery, looting cattle, and burning houses and grain supplies.

The murahalin generally killed all the men they encountered; they killed boys, too, if for no other reason than to prevent them from growing up and being able to defend themselves. Over the course of the twenty-one-year war, some ten thousand young men did just that. Emmanuel Jal was one of them. One day, out of the blue, SPLA soldiers arrived at the seven-year-old's door and took him with them. They told him he was going to receive an education, but their real purpose was to teach him to serve alongside them. A couple years later, Jal officially became an SPLA soldier. In a book he wrote as an adult, Jal tells of the horrors he experienced as a young soldier and the nightmares his experience left him with as an adult.

The day Jal killed many enemy soldiers in the southern Sudan city of Juba proved especially haunting. He wrote,

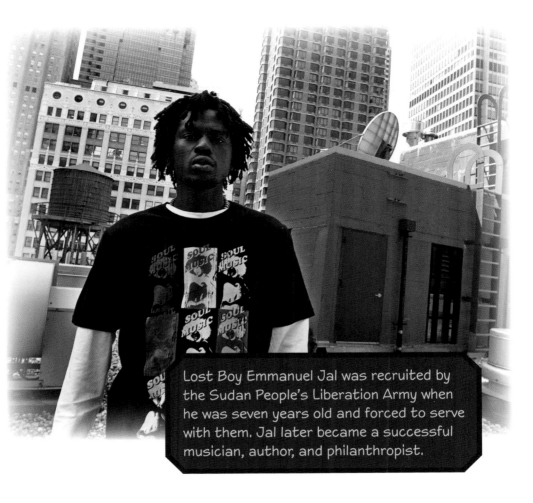

Lost Boy Emmanuel Jal was recruited by the Sudan People's Liberation Army when he was seven years old and forced to serve with them. Jal later became a successful musician, author, and philanthropist.

The day of the raid in Juba was one of the hardest to remember because I had never spoken of it before. I feel no guilt about that day because I took part in killings as the hatred and sorrow built up over years was released in mob violence. I did not kill in cold blood, I killed in war. But that day has tormented me— just as the stories of others have.

The war destroyed many areas of southern Sudan so completely that there was no longer any food for residents

A SUDANESE "WAR CHILD"

Emmanuel Jal is known for more than his history as a Lost Boy and his memoir about being a child soldier in the second Sudanese civil war. His entertainment career is what has given him the most notoriety. When Jal was a refugee, a British aid worker eventually rescued him and snuck him into Kenya. It was there that he began singing, writing songs, and performing concerts for homeless children.

Jal soon recorded some of his songs and became popular in Europe. His song "Gua," which means "power" in Arabic, became the number one song in Kenya and eventually found its way onto an episode of the popular American television show *ER*. His music has won several awards and has helped him to become a spokesperson for several humanitarian organizations, including Amnesty International and his own organization, GUA Africa.

In 2008, a documentary film about Jal's life, *War Child*, was released. The film was a hit with critics and at film festivals. The following year, a book about Jal's life, also called *War Child*, was published. Jal even has a few acting credits, including a role in the film *Blood Diamond*, which stars Leonardo DiCaprio.

to eat. In these instances, fleeing or starving to death were the only options. On one particularly vicious occasion, the murahalin massacred more than one thousand unarmed Dinka refugees, most of whom were burned to death. In another instance, historians Burr and Collins write, the murahalin "surrounded the village the following night, attacking at dawn. Some of the raiders were wearing khaki uniforms.

They herded 170 people, mainly men but also including some women, into a byre [barn] which was then set on fire. Those who escaped were shot. Captives outside the byre then tried to flee but were shot down. Others were thrown down a well and then shot." One Dinka boy said the adults in his village had been burned alive, children old enough to be used as slaves had been taken, and infants too young to travel had been beaten to death.

EXPRESSING THEMSELVES

Once they landed in the United States, many of the Lost Boys turned to writing to express themselves. In 2004, Paterno Onam Chrispino, who was reported to be among the first Lost Boys to graduate from college, wrote a poignant poem about his childhood. It was called "Child Cry of War."

I was found along the road side in open ash air.

I grew up like a child of leach, no mother no father.

I feed on bitter leaves and roots in the desert.

I stay in rain and hot sun for fear.

Are all children in the same condition?

No, a child elsewhere enjoys the calm blue sky,
    and the love of his parent.

A fox has den and a bird has nest, but the child
    of war has nowhere to lay his head for fear of
    bombs and bullets in southern Sudan.

O God lift up this child of war.

The dire situation in southern Sudan did not go unnoticed by the rest of the world. As early as 1980, in response to a multiyear drought that had left many Sudanese starving, the United States had begun sending cash, food, and medical supplies. Aid to Sudan also came from the Red Cross, the United Nations Children's Fund, and Catholic Relief Services. For a variety of reasons—including mismanagement, corruption, poor infrastructure, and heavy rains—getting the aid to where it was needed most often proved difficult. Occasionally, it was almost impossible. The resumption of civil war in 1983 also hampered relief efforts by destroying roads and scattering much of the people from their villages.

Residents at the refugee camp in Kassala, Sudan, rest on bags of supplies delivered by the Red Cross during the famine of 1984–1985.

With people in hiding throughout the region, there was no central location where people could leave—or access—the food. Still, aid workers continued to try.

A 1988 U.S. government report summed up the food situation in southern Sudan at the time: "The population of the Southern Region continues to be highly vulnerable to a food emergency. . . . There are reports that food aid is increasingly being used as a tool for the control of civilians. . . . Relief vehicles have been commandeered for military use. . . . Newspaper correspondents continue to report massive exploitation for Southerners."

In December 1989, former U.S. president Jimmy Carter stepped in to help the Sudanese. He attempted to mediate a peace settlement between the northern government and the Southern Sudan Liberation Movement. But the talks quickly broke down, and no settlement was reached. Meanwhile, the civil war, then well into its sixth year, raged on.

Roughly 3,500 hungry, frightened, and weak Lost Boys arrive at Nasir in southern Sudan in 2002. They had walked from Itang Refugee Camp in Ethiopia.

RUNNING FOR REFUGE

Ethiopia. Though he had no idea at the time, that is where David Bol headed when he scrambled away from his village in 1987. Bol's village had been his world. He knew little or nothing about what existed outside it. He did not know people spoke other languages. He had never heard of other countries. Yet now, at eight years old, he was heading toward a new country. Sometimes his guide was the lone person in his group who knew the way. Other times all he had were directions offered by a stranger.

Day after day, Bol walked barefoot across the unforgiving terrain of southern Sudan. Daytime temperatures often topped 100 degrees Fahrenheit (38 degrees Celsius). The fear of the unknown was constantly with him. He said,

> You're so afraid and you're scared. You just
> run in a direction and you don't know whether
> you're going to survive, if you're going to die
> or how long it's going to take to get there

or what kind of people you're going to find there. At the same time you're thinking about your life, you know, 'cause if you stayed in the village, you're gonna die like the people who are already dead, so the only option was to get out and leave and see what happens.

What happened to Bol during his trek is difficult to describe with words, and even harder to comprehend. Typical days would consist of resting on blankets in the shade of the forest and eating—whatever could be found, including wild grasses of little nutritional value—during the hottest part of the day. Lost Boy Daniel Khoch talked about the hardships he faced on the trek from his village to Ethiopia:

> There was no water and foods for people to drink and eat for three and a half days. As a result, again, we drank our own urine so that to sustain our life. If we were not drunk our own urine and eat soft mud and strange foods, therefore, automatically, we would have died like the rest of the colleagues. . . . The foods we ate during the desert . . . included dry skin from cows, sheep, goats, some dry bones of animals no matter what the animal is. . . . Other desert foods include termites.

Most of the refugees did their walking at night because it was cooler and made it easier to hide. Walking at night became an art. The refugees held hands and formed a human chain to help guide their way through blackened forests. Bol said,

> By 6 or 7 we would start walking, and you would have to walk for the full night, taking maybe short breaks through the night. Just walk all night long until morning. And there are wild animals, there are hyenas all over the place, lions all over the place . . . there are snakes. There are fallen trees all over the place, you step on it and pierce your foot and you can't

walk and someone has to help you. There are no doctors or nurses so if you're injured it's very difficult.

During the four months it took him to reach Ethiopia, Bol became familiar with the sights, sounds, and even smells of death. They were everywhere. "People got eaten by lions and all that stuff," he said. Starving people from his group often would attempt to give up. They would confess that they could not go on any longer, but the group would encourage them to keep walking. If no one could convince them to continue, they would lie down on the side of the road and die. Other refugees would take the belongings of the dead—if they had any—and attempt to sell or trade them for whatever they could get. Sometimes it might be water. Other times it might be a few pieces of corn. Some groups gave responsible older children the task of burying the bodies of their fellow travelers in shallow, hand-dug graves.

The body of a famine victim lies on the ground in southwestern Sudan in 1998. Scenes like this were a common sight for many Lost Boys.

Bol described the scene along the journey:

> It was real difficult having to travel for a couple of months [with] no food, feed[ing] on everything you could find. It was tough and a lot of people died in the wages of hunger or thirst and all that stuff. You see all people lying down on the side of the road dead, eaten by vultures and all that stuff and you witness [this] and you [think], "OK, am I the next?" The next person to go? And you're just hoping you're not next and you keep walking because you have no options. You can't go back, the only way is to just go forward.

The refugees' goals were short-term and straightforward: Make it to a town. Any town. Find something to eat and drink there. Find someone to nurse the wounds of the injured. Survive to do it again. Sometimes people they encountered along the way would lie about which direction the refugees should travel. Go that way, they would say, and you will find a town full of food and water. The refugees would follow, yet when they arrived at the suggested spot, there would be no town. These liars had their own agendas. Exactly what they were was not always easy to tell. Perhaps they wanted the food for themselves. Maybe they supported the government. The refugees soon learned to be skeptical of advice they received, and often they simply ignored it and followed the path they already were on.

There were kind people along the way, too. Some would offer the travelers corn and water. Enough generous people existed that large numbers of refugees made it to Ethiopia. Roughly four months and 1,000 miles (1,609 km) after they began their journey, Bol and his group crossed the swift Gilo River and entered Ethiopia. According to government estimates, some eight thousand boys like Bol died en route.

Tens of thousands of older refugees died, too. But the constant running appeared to be over.

A New Kind of Desperation

The desperation that Bol experienced while traveling across sub-Saharan Sudan did not completely disappear when he made it to Ethiopia. It only changed. Even when aid began coming in, the sheer number of refugees at Bol's camp made it difficult to find enough food to feed everyone. There was no abundance of food and water, which was the dream that had motivated many of the travelers to go on during their most desperate days. The exact number of people in Bol's refugee camp is unknown, but there were thousands. Official estimates reported 350,000 southern Sudanese refugees living in Ethiopia by 1989, the year after Bol arrived. At around the same time, tens of thousands of others showed up in the neighboring countries of Kenya and Uganda.

Lost Boys gather around tents in June 1992 at a refugee camp in Kenya.

Valentino Achak Deng's arrival in Ethiopia is mentioned in Dave Eggers's novel, *What Is the What: The Autobiography of Valentino Achak Deng*. In the book, which is a blend of fact and fiction, Deng says:

> There were boys spread all over the land, and all that was left to do, for some, was to die. The wails came from everywhere. In the quiet of the night, over the hum of the crickets and frogs, there were the screams and moans, spreading over the camp like a storm. It was as if so many of the boys had been waiting to rest, and now that they had settled at Pinyudo [Refugee Camp], their bodies gave out. Boys died of malaria, of dysentery, of snake bites, of scorpion stings. Other illnesses were never named. We were in Ethiopia and there were too many of us.

Refugee camps were riddled with problems. In his book *The Lost Boys of Sudan: An American Story of the Refugee Experience*, author Mark Bixler writes, "[The camps] were desperate places. Flies buzzed around the faces of listless boys and girls with the protruding bellies of the starving and arms that were little more than skin stretched tight over bone."

The Ethiopian camps did have many relative upsides, however. Most important, the refugees' arrival marked an end to their constant walking. The people in charge of the camp, chiefly employees of the United Nations, provided some clothing and food, and there was security against attacks by the Sudanese government. There was a nearby river for fishing. And there were schools, in which children studied subjects such as math and English. Though the education was basic, at least they finally were getting one. Education was important to the southern Sudanese, yet rarely had it been available to them. Other western Ethiopian relief camps, such as those at Dimma and Itang, were similar to the one at Pinyudo.

May 21, 1991, was the beginning of the end of the relative stability that the refugee camps offered the southern Sudanese. On this day, the Ethiopian government, led by hard-line Marxist president Mengistu Haile Mariam, was overthrown. The old government had supported the Sudan People's Liberation Army—many members of which were living in Ethiopian refugee camps—but the new regime did not. In Ethiopia, fights began to break out between the SPLA and the country's new regime. The refugees were no longer welcome in Ethiopia. Hundreds of thousands of refugees soon began returning to their home country of Sudan, where their former miseries and fear awaited them.

David Bol stayed in Ethiopia for a little while after the government's overthrow. Then he, too, finally fled the country. When it came time for him to leave, his group made its way back to the banks of the Gilo River, located at the Ethiopia-Sudan border. Violence surrounded the river. Fighters from the SPLA, the government of Sudan, and the Southern Sudan Independence Movement were shooting and killing. To get back to Sudan, the refugees had to cross the river. So they did. "Hundreds and hundreds, maybe thousands, were trying to cross at the same time," Bol said. "This river is really running fast. If you jumped in and you didn't know how to swim you would drown. There were rocks, too, so if you hit the rocks you were gone. People died. People were there with guns." The river was filled with crocodiles.

Bol made it across the river alive, and he spent a couple months living at a refugee camp just inside the border of southern Sudan. For a while, there was no food available there. The aid agencies that had been assisting the refugees in Ethiopia had not yet arrived at the new site. Fishing and foraging, the refugees ate anything they could find. Some people traveled into nearby villages and offered themselves up for work in exchange for food. Then the Sudanese government discovered the camp's whereabouts and began bombing it. The Red Cross eventually arrived and erected a huge banner for the planes to read. According to Bol, "It said, 'This is a refugee camp,' but they would still go ahead and bomb it. We were lucky enough that [the bombs] were missing the camp." It soon became clear that it was again time to move on.

This time, the refugees were crammed into the covered backs of hundreds of Red Cross trucks and driven across the hot desert to Kenya. Bol vividly remembers the trek:

> They sealed the whole [back of the truck]. So you're in something toasted. It's over 100 degrees and people are sweating from the top to the bottom. You can't even turn around because it's so filled up. You can't even breathe. There's nothing they can do because the militia would wait for us and if they see the people being transported and that it's not goods or food, they would shoot through the trucks. It was terrible.

Lost Boys often were transported in the backs of covered trucks like this one used to evacuate refugees from a camp in Adjumani, Uganda, in 1989.

Unlike the refugees' nighttime trek on foot to Ethiopia, the Red Cross trucks drove during the heat of the day, when the militias were at rest. The trucks stopped at night so the refugees could sleep on the ground of the open desert. Thirteen-year-old Bol had injured his leg, so he rode in one of the last trucks of the convoy. Since his truck arrived at the sleeping area later than others, he always slept near the outside of the group of refugees. One night, when the militia arrived and started randomly shooting, Bol's sleeping position almost cost him his life. He was shot in the back. "Then the militia just ran away," he said.

Bol was driven to a small-town hospital, which could not do much for him other than bandage his wounds. He was then placed in the back of a truck and driven to a better-equipped Red Cross hospital in Kenya. En route, a severely wounded patient lying next to him in the truck died. Bol said, "I was just looking at him and said, 'OK, maybe I'll be the next one.'" The truck stopped long enough to bury the dead boy alongside the road. "They asked me if I knew who he was," Bol said, "but I didn't know his name."

In most respects, John Bul Dau's story is the same as Bol's, but the specifics vary. Dau was thirteen when soldiers attacked his Dinka village in the middle of the night in 1987. He ended up fleeing the village with his best friend's father. The pair headed east toward Ethiopia. As they walked, their group grew larger. Militia members beat them along the way, and they were constantly hungry. Many in Dau's group died during the trip. One time Dau was so thirsty that he drank another man's urine. At the end of the year, Dau's group made it to a refugee camp in Ethiopia.

Dau's camp, like Bol's, was far from perfect. Many of the refugees there died from cholera—an infection of the small intestine that they got from drinking dirty water. Whooping cough, chicken pox, and measles also were prevalent.

UNITED NATIONS HIGH COMMISSIONER FOR REFUGEES

Wherever there has been war, there have been civilians trying to get out of the danger zone. The sheer brutality of experiences such as the Russian campaign of 1941 to 1944 and the Japanese invasion of China in the 1930s made one thing clear to the Allied powers that won the World War II: in addition to bringing to justice people who committed crimes against humanity, someone had to help the immense civilian populations that had suffered those atrocities.

Established in 1950, the United Nations High Commissioner for Refugees (UNHCR) was just that agency. The UNHCR is dedicated to protecting the rights of refugees worldwide. One of those rights is to seek refuge, either within your own country or in another country, if you are being persecuted for religious, political, or other reasons. The UNHCR has done a lot of work in relatively unstable developing countries, such as Sudan, Ethiopia, and Uganda, the latter of which both received and generated refugees.

The UNHCR had plenty of work to do after World War II, a devastating conflict that left millions homeless. The immediate start of the Cold War, between the communist countries of Eastern Europe and the Western democracies, also gave rise to large refugee populations, which headed to the United States and Western Europe.

In 1954, the UNHCR won the Nobel Peace Prize in recognition of its work with refugees in Europe, and in 1981 it won the award again for its efforts worldwide. The UNHCR has been at every site of major conflict since its founding, including

Eastern Europe in the 1950s, Southeast Asia in the 1960s and 1970s, Afghanistan, Africa, Iraq, and beyond. Currently, the UNHCR says there are more than 34 million refugees or potential refugees on its watch list. The majority of these people live in Africa.

Looking ahead, the UNHCR's number one goal is the physical security of refugees. The growing problem of human trafficking can lead to other problems such as slavery and genocide—especially as countries tighten their immigration and asylum policies. The responsibility for fixing these problems always has been in the hands of the individual countries involved. But for sixty years, as an international conscience, the UNHCR has been there.

The United Nations eventually showed up with food, medicine, and other supplies. But many people died before help arrived.

In May 1991, the month when the Ethiopian government was overthrown, Ethiopian soldiers attacked Dau's camp. His escape story is nearly identical to Bol's. As the soldiers opened fire on the unarmed refugees, Dau ran to the nearby Gilo River and made the difficult swim across it. Dau said,

> Perhaps 20,000 Sudanese boys went into the Gilo River that day. Nobody knows how many died in the crossing. Maybe 2,000, maybe 3,000, maybe more. Some drowned. Some caught a bullet or shell fragment. Some found their way into a crocodile's belly. I know the crocs had a feast, because others who made it to the western shore told me they had seen their friends in the beasts' cold jaws. One man showed me the stump of his hand and told me a crocodile bit it off while he swam.

Dau was not injured in the crossing. He made it back to his homeland and eventually made the trek on to Kenya.

The majority of the refugees who fled Ethiopia ended up at Kakuma Refugee Camp. Located in the northwest corner of Kenya, Kakuma was some 60 miles (97 km) from the Sudan-Kenya border. The environment there was harsh and not conducive to any type of farming that might offer the refugees long-term sustenance. All food had to be brought in. Temperatures at Kakuma averaged 104 degrees F (40 degrees C) in the daytime, and poisonous scorpions, spiders, and snakes were everywhere. There was no water on-site—each day, women and children walked for miles to gather it.

The camp, which began as just a few tents, soon swelled to miles and miles of cardboard houses and mud huts. Perhaps the name of the region best sums up what it had to offer. In Swahili, a prominent language spoken in Africa, *kakuma* means "nowhere."

The Kakuma Refugee Camp was run by the Red Cross and the United Nations High Commissioner for Refugees (UNHCR). In late 1992, Kakuma sheltered roughly 11,000 Lost Boys—some as young as four—and close to 20,000 people overall. According to an article in *Refugee Magazine*,

> Many [of the boys were] abducted from their families at a very early age by Sudanese rebel forces looking for replacements and for cannon fodder to send through mine fields. The boys are among the worst cases ever seen by UNHCR. Many of them suffer from deep depression, refusing to play, to go to school or even to get out of bed in the morning. They spend their days doing nothing. A UNHCR specialist working with the boys says the terror they have experienced is deeply engraved in their subconscious and has resurfaced now that they are safe.

Similar but smaller camps existed elsewhere in Kenya, as well as in other nearby countries such as Uganda.

The majority of the Lost Boys spent several years at Kakuma. Eventually, the camp became their home. Many of them ended up living there longer—and safer—than they had ever lived anywhere else, including their home villages.

Upon arrival at Kakuma, refugees were required to register with the people in charge. The staff then gave the refugees identification cards that listed their name, date of birth (in some cases this had to be a best guess), birthplace, date of arrival, and parents' names (if known). One of the goals of the identification procedure was to help reunite family members. Many times, people from the same family were living at the same site and did not know it.

Most of the Lost Boys were in terrible shape, both physically and mentally, when they arrived at Kakuma. One psychologist called them "one of the most traumatized groups

SCHOOL FOR REFUGEES

"Education is my mother and father." This six-word saying became the motto of the Lost Boys, who had been taught from a young age that only through education could they ever hope to escape their perilous situation. But what was life at school really like for the refugees? Here is a summary of the daily routine at Gilo Preparatory School at Kakuma Refugee Camp in Kenya. The school is for children ages five and six.

At 8 a.m., children are greeted at the gate to the school to start their day. A bell rings, and the children gather for a parade. They learn what they will be doing that day. They are checked for hygiene, which includes examining their fingernails and clothes. After inspection, they move on to class and study subjects such as reading and writing.

At 10 a.m., there is a snack break and a thirty-minute recess. Then the students return to class and resume their studies.

At 12:30 p.m., school breaks due to the intense midday heat. It resumes around 3 p.m. and continues for approximately another hour. The children then return to their individual villages.

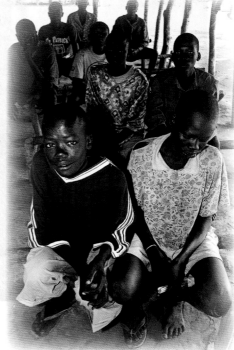

Due to a lack of funding for supplies, the students write on chalk slates. They erase the slate every time it is filled, so their work is never saved. The school has two classes of sixty children each.

of children I have ever met." The boys suffered flashbacks to the times when their villages were attacked. In their minds, they would relive the horrors they had faced during their long and treacherous walks across the countryside. Sometimes they would hear the screams of those who had been injured or killed along the way. There were valid reasons for the boys' mental anguish. Surveys conducted by workers at Kakuma found that 74 percent of the Lost Boys had survived shootings or bombings. Eighty-five percent had seen someone starve to death. Ninety-two percent had been shot at. And almost all of the Lost Boys—97 percent—had seen someone killed by war.

The camp's identification system worked in some instances. Many Lost Boys were reunited with family members at Kakuma. Beny Ngor Chol was one of the fortunate ones. "I couldn't believe it," he said. "I was just leaving the UNHCR office where I'd been helping sort papers. Someone tapped me on the shoulder. I turned but didn't recognize the young woman looking at me. 'Do you know you are related to my family?' she said and held her arms out wide. Then I realized she was my mother's niece. Her eyes are so like my mama's. I burst into tears and we hugged each other. She was crying too."

For others, fellow refugees became their new family. Many of the Lost Boys who became friends at Kakuma remained close for a long time, and some eventually lived in the same cities in the United States. Yet in the camp's atmosphere of communal survival, fights often broke out, most commonly between members of the Dinka and Nuer tribes, in part because of issues between members of the Southern Sudan Independence Movement and the Sudan People's Liberation Army.

The civil war, which had been going on for years outside the camps, continued. Even wars outside Africa directly impacted Sudan. For example, when the Sudanese government chose to side with Iraq after Iraq invaded Kuwait in 1990, Sudan fell out of favor with several countries—including Egypt, Great

Britain, and the United States—that had been providing support and trying to help end Sudan's civil war.

In addition, the Sudanese government provided sanctuary and assistance to the leaders of many terrorist organizations, including a Saudi Arabian man named Osama bin Laden. From 1991 to 1996, bin Laden had given aid to Sudan in exchange for the government's assistance to al Qaida, his terrorist group. For this and other reasons, the United States declared Sudan an official sponsor of terrorism in 1993. Four years later, the U.S. government imposed sanctions against Sudan, and, in 1998, the U.S. military bombed at least one suspected terrorist site in Sudan.

For a while, the attention that much of the world community had been giving to the Lost Boys' plight took a back seat to these and other issues. In 1998, however, a new philanthropic movement began to build in the United States: the idea of allowing some of the Lost Boys to resettle there. While the United States has a long history of opening its doors to refugees, relatively few had come from Africa.

From left, Lost Boys Abraham Malok, Elijah Maluk, John Lueth, and Abraham Madhler stand in their apartment in Fargo, North Dakota, in 2004.

Some humanitarians raised concerns about the idea. Although giving refugees an opportunity to live in a technologically advanced, wealthy country may seem like a generous act, it has drawbacks. For example, refugees who moved might never find their families, and they would almost certainly lose touch with their culture. But there were positives, too. The Lost Boys' living conditions would improve greatly. They would also be able to receive a good education, which was exactly what most southern Sudanese had always wanted.

In 1999, U.S. leaders decided to allow approximately 3,800 refugees from Kakuma Refugee Camp to come to the country. This was a relatively small minority of the many millions of people who had been displaced, but many people still saw it as a positive gesture. To be eligible, the refugees truly had to be Lost Boys. They had to be among the 28,000 original boys who had lost their parents, had fled their homes as a result of civil war, and had made the dangerous treks from Sudan to Ethiopia back to Sudan and eventually to Kakuma.

Many refugees who did not meet the U.S. government's criteria attempted to qualify by making up stories of the hardships they had faced in getting to Kakuma. Those who were caught were disqualified from the program. It is unknown how many, if any, refugees were able to lie their way to the United States. One thing is certain: there was no shortage of people who were willing to leave Kakuma behind for the unknown in America. That is still the case today.

The selected Lost Boys attended classes on what to expect when they arrived in their new country. Most of what they learned involved basic aspects of everyday life that people in most countries take for granted. The Lost Boys learned about electricity and how it worked. They learned about how to get a driver's license. They learned about telephones, which were uncommon in southern Sudan. Their teachers also stressed the importance of obtaining and holding onto a job.

According to author Mark Bixler, the Lost Boys were "overwhelmed" by the information they received. "Most had never ridden in a car," Bixler writes, "let alone considered the need for a driver's license. Most had never read a newspaper, and so the concept of classified ads floated in an abstract realm. For young men who had never worked in a wage economy, talk of salary deductions and benefits may as well have been written in Latin."

The tough learning curve did little to quell the Lost Boys' excitement. Each day, beginning in fall 2000, they traveled from every last corner of the camp to check for their names on a public board. If their name was listed, they had been selected to go to the United States. David Bol remembers the joyous day when he saw his name on the list. He soon found out that he had been sponsored by the Catholic Church to go to Seattle, Washington. He described his feelings on that day:

Lost Boy Emmanuel Makender, center, eats dinner with his foster family in Hudsonville, Michigan, in January 2001. Makender's foster family, the Kroghs, included, from left, Lois, Susannah, Derek, Kyle, and Jacob.

It was a joy, it was tears and happiness and everything just flying in your head. It was also excitement. You didn't know what to expect, where are you going to, what are you going to find up there? It was a lot of stuff going in your head. Like the friends, the people that you knew you're going to leave them behind, maybe you're not going to see them again. Will you be able to come back again to Sudan? What is United States? What is it, you know? What are you going to find? Just a lot of things inside your head, but I was excited because I knew that all these hard struggles, all these difficult things would be left behind and I would move on and try to experience a new life again where you didn't have to worry about wars or fighting. If it turns out to be bad, we'll just handle it the same way we've handled everything that we've gone through.

John Bul Dau's excitement was equally high when he discovered he had made the cut. He said, "I was very, very happy. I jumped and skipped as I ran home. I didn't know when I would go, or what city I would fly to, but I didn't care. . . . Of course, the boys who received letters of refusal felt very sad. A few went crazy. Others had a bad case of sour grapes. They told me that when I got to America, I would not get a very good job. I would have to cook for my wife—an embarrassment to a Dinka man—or maybe get a job cleaning up dog poop." One woman told him, "We hear that in the United States, you don't know your brother, you don't know your cousin. You forget your family, and you will not send us money here. We have heard from those who have gone to America before you. . . . They are not sending money back; they are not good Dinka."

The negativity did not diminish Dau's excitement. After all, he was on his way to America.

God Grew Tired of Us, a 2006 award-winning documentary film, was partially based on the life of Lost Boy John Bul Dau.

COMING TO AMERICA

David Bol's plane landed at Seattle-Tacoma International Airport in Washington State in June 2001. After years of suffering in his home country of Sudan, the Lost Boy finally was in a place where life would be easier. The challenges of adjusting to his new environment only made him laugh. For example, the chilly, unpredictable weather of the Pacific Northwest gave him fits, especially when the season changed to winter. Bol and the other resettled Lost Boys soon had their first experiences with snow. Bol said,

> We asked people, "What is that?" and they said, "That's the snow." And you can see people laying outside, kids coming to church and families playing in the snow but we were just sitting inside saying, "Why are they playing in that cold thing? No way!" So we would just be wrapped up in our blankets looking through the windows seeing all the kids excited, playing and throwing snow and all that stuff and I was like, "Are they crazy? Why are they playing outside, that thing is too cold."

Even drinking water directly out of a refrigerator or eating ice cream proved too cold for Bol to handle. On one occasion, he had to throw an ice cream cone away because his body could not handle eating it.

Bol's first job in the United States—and his first wage-earning job ever—was as a housekeeper at a hotel near the airport. But the job proved too strenuous on his back, which still was injured from the gunshot wound he had received nine years earlier. Due to that and other injuries he had received in Africa, Bol could no longer lift heavy items. So he quit his housekeeping job and found a less strenuous job as an airport security guard.

Work was not the only activity that occupied Bol's time, however. He never forgot the real reason he was in the United States: to continue his education. Each day he worked a twelve-hour shift as a security guard, from 6 p.m. until 6 a.m. After work he attended a community college to study for his general equivalency diploma (GED), which is the equivalent of a high school diploma. Bol soon passed his tests and earned his GED.

His GED allowed Bol to achieve his next goal: to go to college full-time. But he struggled with the idea. He recently had begun communicating with his family, after he had discovered they were living near the Sudan-Uganda border. Like most resettled Lost Boys, Bol immediately began sending his family money to help support them. Attending school full-time would not allow him to make enough money to continue helping his family while paying his bills and tuition. So instead of going to college, Bol enrolled in a Job Corps program and trained as a pharmacy technician. He now works for a major drugstore chain in Moses Lake, Washington, and takes classes at Big Bend Community College. His goal is to transfer to a university to earn his college degree.

John Bul Dau arrived in America from Kakuma two months after Bol. Dau's new home of Syracuse, New York,

Lost Boy John Bul Dau, shown here in Park City, Utah, in 2007, eventually returned to Sudan to help start a medical clinic that has since treated more than 30,000 people.

was on the opposite side of the country from Bol's, but the two men went through similar initial experiences. Dau's first major shock, which happened as he was leaving a New York airport, involved automobiles. First, he was stunned by the fact that his female caseworker would be the person driving him to where he was staying. In his area of Africa, women were not allowed to drive. Second, he was equally amazed that the caseworker actually *owned* the car she was driving. That never would have happened in his homeland.

American roads also astounded Dau. He said, "I had only seen city streets in Kenya, bumpy with potholes that jolted cars and slowed the patterns of traffic. And southern Sudan had only dirt paths between the villages. They looked nothing like the wide, velvet black ribbons that curled and ducked and flowed as far as I could see."

The act of shopping for groceries was also shocking for Dau. As he made his way through an American store for the first time, he had no idea what most of the goods were. This was especially true in the store's seafood section. Dau said,

Clams, lobsters, shrimp—do people eat such things? Yes? I didn't want to criticize, but they . . .looked like big bugs. Someone asked if I liked fish. I said no. That wasn't true; I do eat fish. But I didn't want to eat anything that came from the counter next to the giant insects. Not far away, I saw lots of chicken roasting on skewers. I wanted to eat those chickens.

As it had been for Bol, seeing snow for the first time also was a major event for Dau.

Dau's first job in the United States was loading boxes. He then moved on to various other jobs, including working the late shift as a cook at McDonald's. Like Bol, Dau sent much of the money he earned to friends and family in Sudan. In 2002, Dau enrolled at Onondaga Community College in Syracuse, and eventually he transferred to Syracuse University.

In 2006, Dau returned to Sudan as the leader of a project aimed at building a medical clinic in his home village. When the award-winning documentary film *God Grew Tired of Us* was released in 2006, Dau's story received a lot of attention from the national media because the movie was based partially on his life story. Dau had coauthored a book of the same name. His dream of bringing a clinic to his home country was realized in May 2007, when the Duk Lost Boys Clinic opened in southern Sudan. The clinic has since provided care to more than 30,000 people.

Other Lost Boys ended up scattered in various states. Texas received 265 of them, the most of any state. By comparison, Mississippi received only five Lost Boys, while just one ended up in Washington, D.C.

Regardless of where they landed, not all Lost Boys adjusted as well to life in the United States as did David Bol and John Bul Dau. Many struggled with their new living situations. For example, those who were under eighteen when they arrived in the country were placed in foster homes and allowed to go to school and to get their diploma for free. Those who were over the age of eighteen were given free places to live for ninety days but then left to fend for themselves. Some managed to find jobs, get their GEDs, and eventually go to college. Others, such as Santino Majok Chuor, simply worked.

Chuor was twenty-one years old when he arrived in Houston, Texas, in 2001. He was too old to attend high school. He tried to work during the day and study during the evening, but he found it too difficult. Chuor sent a large portion of his wages to his disabled brother in Sudan. He said, "I did not manage to go to school because I could not find the time. There's no way out unless you get education."

Chuor also commented that his transition to the United States was difficult because he was not specifically told what the process would be like:

> [W]e were not told that we would be staying here as independents, responsible for your own schooling and your own life. They said that when you come to the United States there is someone who will take care of your education and your living. There would be a sponsor who would visit you every week and see how you are living and how your education is going. When we came here, the agency supported us only three months. And after three months, they said that you had to look after yourself. You were responsible for your own life at that point. They did not tell us before. That confused us because we didn't know the particulars of living here, like how to get into a school or the levels of the class that you should go to in comparison with our schooling in Africa.

Chuor has since been granted the opportunity to attend

college, thanks to the donation of one viewer of *God Grew Tired of Us*, in which his story also was featured.

Lost Boy Isaac Majak also struggled as he adjusted to his new life in the United States. After a visit to Sudan in 2005, he dropped out of college so he could work more to send more money home. At one point, the money Majak made in the United States was supporting seventeen people in Sudan. He worked as many as 112 hours a week and slept an average of 3 hours a day.

According to African culture expert Dianna Shandy, people in many parts of Africa perceive the United States as a utopia. This perception can create disappointment for people who eventually emigrate there, as the Lost Boys did. Said Shandy,

> [Many refugees] start out at less than zero here. It's an incredible uphill battle. Sometimes when there are connections between [the United States] and people who are still in Africa, when they call back and talk about their lives they don't necessarily tell people, I went off and I got this incredible opportunity to go to America and my life is really crummy. So I think sometimes there is a representation of life here in America that's better than how refugees actually live and those images and notions get communicated back home, so then the people who come later have expectations about something that's a bit idealized.

Because of this idealization, people in Sudan often place large amounts of pressure on the Lost Boys to send money home. One Lost Boy said,

> Some of the guys in Africa, when they hear that you are in the U.S., they call you, asking for money and a lot of things. But you have no job and are almost being chased out of the apartment. People think that the U.S. has

everything. So when you say that you don't have something, they cannot accept it and call you a bad person. I feel guilty, you know, I cannot support my people back home even though I try as much as I can. But it is very difficult here.

The September 11, 2001, terrorist attacks on the United States also negatively impacted many of the Lost Boys. Almost immediately following the attacks—in which nearly three thousand people died—the U.S. government placed the blame on Osama bin Laden and his terrorist organization, al Qaida. Both the group and its leader had been associated with Sudan. Although bin Laden's association had been with Muslims in northern Sudan, and the Lost Boys were from the non-Muslim southern part of the country, some of the Lost Boys still suffered discrimination in the United States. Shortly after the attacks, one Lost Boy living in Boston said, "The worst thing that happened to us was when Sudan was associated with Osama bin Laden. It brought a bad record for us. Yet people don't know that there has been a twenty-year war between the north and the south. The north is forcing the south to become Muslim and we refuse that. It is older people who know what is happening in Sudan."

Changing Times

In many ways, conditions in Sudan have changed since the first wave of Lost Boys began landing in the United States in 2001. The civil war, which drove the boys from their villages, more or less came to an end in January 2005, with the signing of a peace treaty between the Sudanese government and the Sudan People's Liberation Movement. The agreement called for a permanent cease-fire between the north and the south, as well as the withdrawal of troops from southern Sudan.

The nation's new, temporary constitution declared,

ONE LOST BOY'S TRAGIC TALE

One of the saddest stories of a Lost Boy who made it to the United States is that of John Bior Deng. Deng initially moved to Texas from his Kenyan refugee camp. On July 24, 2009, he got in a fight with a man outside a bar in Iowa City, Iowa. When police arrived on the scene, they found that the man fighting with Deng had been stabbed. According to police, Deng continued fighting and made a threatening gesture with a knife toward the other man. That is when a policeman shot and killed Deng.

At the time he was killed, Deng was twenty-six years old and had been homeless for an undisclosed period of time. Once it was discovered that Deng was a Lost Boy, his case received a lot of media coverage. There were some reports that Deng may not have even had a knife and that the officer had been mistaken in shooting him. However, after an official investigation into the case, authorities determined that the officer was justified in killing Deng.

The Republic of the Sudan is a sovereign, democratic, decentralized, multicultural, multiracial, multiethnic, multireligious, and multilingual State; committed to the respect and promotion of human dignity and founded on justice, equality and the advancement of human rights and freedoms. It is an all embracing homeland wherein races and cultures coalesce and religions co-exist in harmony.

In a major coup, former SPLM leader John Garang was named vice president of Sudan. Less than a month later, however, he died in a helicopter crash that some believed was suspicious. The government has been slow to implement the policies and programs agreed to in 2005, but much progress has been made.

Sudan still is not entirely peaceful, however. In 2003, a large war broke out in the Darfur region of western Sudan. In 2009, fighting began in Sudan's Abyei region, an oil-rich area located between the north and the south. The nation's 2010 elections were fraught with controversy. In January 2011, the south held a referendum on secession from the north, and an overwhelming majority of southern Sudan's citizens decided to secede. Based on that vote, South Sudan became its own country.

The more than 2 million people killed over the course of the second Sudanese civil war died by famine, disease, or violence. Some 4 million southern Sudanese were displaced within Sudan, and roughly 600,000 became refugees in other countries. Even five years after the end of the war, less than half the refugees had returned to southern Sudan. Thousands of people remain at Kakuma Refugee Camp in Kenya, where many of the Lost Boys spent large portions of their formative years.

Nonetheless, the end of the civil war provided the Lost Boys with an opportunity to return to their country. Since then, some have permanently returned to southern Sudan to marry and to raise families. Sometimes they married girlfriends whom they had left behind in order to move to the United States. A large majority of the original Lost Boys still permanently live in the United States. Many, such as John Bul Dau, have returned to help improve conditions in their homeland, however. Here are some examples of Lost Boys who settled in Syracuse, New York, and have worked to benefit Sudan:

Daniel Garang Amet raised money for and played a major role in the drilling of two wells and the building of a clinic in his home village of Malakal. His goal, he said, is to allow the next generation of Sudanese women to have their children in hospitals rather than in the bush, the way he was born.

Gabriel Bol Deng aided in the drilling of six wells and

THE DARFUR CONFLICT

While the Sudanese civil war still was under way, a separate conflict broke out in 2003 in the Darfur region of western Sudan. This happened after two antigovernment groups demanded a greater share of the country's resources and an end to nomadic bandits' raids on the area's villages.

Since that time, the Sudanese government has come under fierce criticism for its support of the Janjaweed, a militia group said to be responsible for mass atrocities including murder and rape. Bringing security to Darfur has been difficult for many reasons, such as the sheer size of the area. Darfur is about the size of the state of Texas, the second-biggest American state. Meanwhile, Sudan is approximately the size of one-third of the United States.

Despite the twin handicaps of poverty and remote locations, the splintered and divided Darfurian rebel groups have carried the fight to the government—including at least one military attack on Sudan's capital, Khartoum. What captured international attention, however, was the horrific violence against civilians, largely at the hands of government-backed forces. Though the numbers are contested, an estimated 300,000 people have died and more than 2 million have become refugees as a result of the Darfur conflict, which has continued to rage on and off despite several internationally brokered cease-fires. In many ways, the situation in Darfur is similar to the conflict between the north and the south in the Sudanese civil wars.

Since 2005, the United Nations has documented human rights abuses and crimes against humanity in the Darfur conflict. This documentation has led to war crimes charges against a number of Sudanese government officials—including, in 2008, charges of genocide and crimes against humanity against Sudanese president Omar al-Bashir. The government of Sudan has held a number of trials of Janjaweed members and government officials accused of war crimes, but critics say the government has only done this to avoid facing the World Court in the Netherlands.

In 2006, the first elements of a joint United Nations–African Union peacekeeping force, UNAMID, entered the country. Lack of cooperation from the Khartoum government hampered full deployment of UNAMID forces, however. As of 2011, some 22,000 soldiers and policemen from more than forty countries were stationed in Darfur and were attempting to provide security for the civilian population and humanitarian groups operating there.

raised money to build a school—which, he specified, girls must be allowed to attend—in his home village of Arirang.

Angelo Ngong Kiir raised money to build a clinic, an orphanage, and a school in his home village of Wunlang.

And the list goes on. Hundreds more Lost Boys contribute silently, most frequently by sending money from each of their paychecks to relatives in southern Sudan.

David Bol seriously began thinking about returning to his homeland in 2007, the year he became a U.S. citizen. That same year, he spoke at the U.S. Department of Labor's national Job Corps convention in Washington, D.C. Bol has not yet returned to Sudan, but he plans to do so once he gets his passport. He badly wants to see his family, which currently lives just south of Sudan in Uganda. "They are crying all the time," Bol said, "because they don't even know what I look like."

Today, the thirty-two-year-old Bol sometimes teaches

Many of the Lost Boys of Sudan received a fair amount of publicity when they arrived in the United States. In addition to the Lost Boys, many other Sudanese-born people have made an international impact for other reasons. Here are just a few.

Manute Bol, a former NBA basketball player, immigrated to the United States in 1982. Standing 7 feet, 7 inches (2.3 meters) tall, Bol was at one time the tallest player in NBA history. He played a total of ten seasons for four different teams, and after leaving the game he contributed nearly all of his money to charitable causes in Sudan. He died of kidney failure in 2010.

Supermodel Alek Wek was born in Sudan in 1977. The seventh of nine children, Wek fled the country in the middle of the second Sudanese civil war and went to London, where an agent discovered her at a street fair and signed her to a modeling contract. She has since worked for many major names in the fashion business, including Gap, Ralph Lauren, Jean Paul Gaultier, Coach, and Banana Republic. Like many expatriate Sudanese, she does charity work to benefit her home, as well as working for the U.S. Committee for Refugees advisory council and the United Nations Children's Fund.

Actor Awino Gam was born in Sudan in 1979. One of the Lost Boys, Gam went on to play roles with themes similar to his life—particularly in 2003's *Tears of the Sun*, a Bruce Willis film in which a group of villagers flees ethnic cleansing. Gam is also the author of children's books about his experiences leaving his homeland.

Lost Boy David Bol is shown working at the Columbia Basin Job Corps Center in Moses Lake, Washington, in 2007. "Appreciate that you have the privilege to be in a country like this," Bol tells the American students he now teaches.

others at the same Job Corps program that once helped him. When the opportunity presents itself, he enjoys telling his students about his plight, which took him from abject poverty and near death in his African homeland to his current role as a student, pharmacy technician, and thriving American. His favorite advice to give his students goes something like this:

> You guys should be really proud that you were born in a country like this where you have freedom. You can say whatever you want to say, you have food, you have families around. You can go to school. You can work and all that stuff, you know, you guys should be proud of that and appreciate that you have the privilege to be in a country like this. For most of us, for most of us growing up in a war-torn country—not just in Sudan, even in other countries in Africa—this is what we had to go through, there was nothing, you just have to live day by day, hour by hour. You sleep not knowing if tomorrow you're going to get up or not.

TIME LINE

540—Christianity comes to Sudan

1500s—Followers of the prophet Muhammad bring the religion of Islam to Sudan

1899—Britain and Egypt take joint control of Sudan

1920s—Nationalism sweeps Sudan with the goal of uniting north and south

1955—First civil war begins between northern and southern Sudan

1956—Sudan gains independence

1971—Southern Sudan Liberation Movement created

1972—First civil war ends with Addis Ababa agreement

1983—Second Sudanese civil war begins

1987—Lost Boys begin fleeing villages

1989—Some 1 million southern Sudanese have fled the war-torn south for the northern capital of Khartoum; 350,000 refugees registered in Ethiopia

2001—Roughly 3,800 Lost Boys and Lost Girls resettle in United States

2005—Sudan's second civil war ends

2011—Southern Sudan citizens overwhelmingly vote to secede from northern Sudan; South Sudan becomes its own country

NOTES

Introduction

p. 5, "It sounded like a dream . . . ": Author interview with David Bol.

Chapter 1

p. 10, par. 2, "Some historians estimate . . . ": Helen Chapin Metz, ed., *Sudan: A Country Study* (Washington, D.C.: Library of Congress, 1992), p. 4.

p. 12, sidebar, "It is derived from …," www.ancientsudan.org/ geography_01_alternative_names.htm (accessed July 12, 2010) and "Sudan," www.dictionary.reference.com/browse/Sudan (accessed July 12, 2010).

p. 12, par. 1, "In fact, just five months prior . . . ": Ibid., p. 32.

p. 12, par. 3, "In a pamphlet he wrote . . . ": Joseph Lagu, "Anya-Nya: What We Fight For," 1972, http://theblacklistpub.ning.com/ profiles/ blogs/the-root-causes-of-the-war-in (accessed July 12, 2010).

p. 13, par. 1, "At first poorly armed . . . ": "Sudan: First Civil War," www.globalsecurity.org/military/world/war/sudan-civil-war1.htm (accessed July 14, 2010).

p. 15, par. 1, "As historians J. Millard Burr and Robert O. Collins . . . ": J. Millard Burr and Robert O. Collins, *Requiem for the Sudan: War, Drought & Disaster Relief on the Nile* (Boulder, CO: Westview Press, 1995), p. 7.

p. 16, par. 1, "This time Libya and Ethiopia . . . ": Burr and Collins, p. 17.

p. 16, par. 3, "David Bol remembers . . . ": Author interview with David Bol.

p. 18, par. 2, "By 1989, some one million . . . ": Metz, pp. 243–244.

p. 18, sidebar, "Here is a list …": Compiled by complied by Richard Lobban, November 10, 2010, from the *Dinka Dictionary* by Fr. A. Nebel , F.S.C.J. Published in Wau, Verona Fathers, 1954, and from a version of the same dictionary refined by linguist Roger Blench on December 17, 2005.

p. 19, par. 2, "First, his parents . . . ": John Bul Dau with Michael S. Sweeney, *God Grew Tired of Us: A Memoir* (Washington, D.C.: National Geographic, 2007), pp. 33–34.

Chapter 2

p. 21, par. 1, "David Bol was eight years old . . . ": Author interview with David Bol.

p. 22, par. 3, "Daniel Khoch, for example . . . ": Mark Bixler, *The Lost Boys of Sudan: An American Story of the Refugee Experience* (Athens: The University of Georgia Press, 2005), pp. 57–58.

p. 23, par. 3, "John Chol Kon was only five . . . ": Beverly Naidoo, *Making It Home: Real-Life Stories from Children Forced to Flee* (New York: Dial Books, 2004), p. 88.

p. 24, par. 2, "Some of Sudan's real-life Lost Boys . . . ": Sarah Morrison, "Dave Eggers helps Sudan's 'Lost Boys' get a fresh start at school," *The Guardian*, August 3, 2010, www.guardian. co.uk/ education/2010/aug/03/dave-eggers-sudan-secondary-school (accessed August 5, 2010).

p. 24, par. 2, "Another Lost Boy . . . ": Martin Masumbuko Muhindi and Kiganzi Nyakato, "Integration of the Sudanese 'Lost Boys' in Boston, Massachusetts, U.S.A., 2002," http://web.mit.edu/cis/ www/migration/pubs/Mahindi.pdf (accessed August 1, 2010).

p. 24, par. 3, "Other Lost Boys have found . . . ": Author interview with David Bol.

p. 24, par. 4, "Deng Malou, a Sudanese refugee . . . ": Amanda Gross, "One of Sudan's 'Lost Boys' shares his tale of survival," *The Simmons Voice*, November 5, 2009, http://media.www. thesimmonsvoice.com/media/storage/paper829/news/2009/11/05/ Features/One-Of.Sudans.lost.Boys.Shares.His.Tale. Of.Survival-3822633.shtml (accessed July 25, 2010).

p. 24, par. 1, "Experts in Sudanese culture . . . ": Author interview with Dianna Shandy.

p. 26, sidebar: "Ayen, an eighteen-year-old girl . . . ": Ishbel Matheson, "The 'Lost Girls' of Sudan," *BBC News*, June 7, 2002, http://news.bbc.co.uk/2/hi/africa/2031286.stm (accessed July 25, 2010).

p. 28, par. 2, "One such militia was known . . . ": Metz, p. 257.

p. 28, par. 3, "Emmanuel Jal was one of them . . . ": Emmanuel Jal, *War Child: A Child Soldier's Story* (New York: St. Martin's, 2009), p. 255.

p. 30, par. 1, "In another instance . . . ": Burr and Collins, pp. 106–107.

p. 31, sidebar: Paterno Onam Chrispino, www.lostboyschicago. com/ Writings/PaternoChrispino1.htm (accessed July 30, 2010).

p. 31, par. 1, "One Dinka boy said . . . ": Burr and Collins, pp. 106–107.

p. 33, par. 2, "A 1988 U.S. government report . . . ": Ibid., pp. 111–112.

Chapter 3

p. 35, par. 2, "Day after day, Bol walked . . . ": Author interview with David Bol.

p. 36, par. 2, "Lost Boy Daniel Khoch . . . ": Bixler, p. 59.

p. 36, par. 3, "By 6, or 7 we would . . . ": Author interview with David Bol.

p. 37, par. 2, "It was real difficult . . . ": Author interview with David Bol.

p. 38, par. 4, "According to government estimates . . . ": Bixler, p. 57.

p. 39, par. 2, "Official estimates reported . . . ": www.country-data.com/ cgi-bin/query/r-13440.html (accessed July 28, 2010).

p. 40, par. 1, "Valentino Achak Deng's arrival . . . ": Dave Eggers, *What Is the What*, reproduced at www.npr.org/templates/story/story. php?storyId=6412768 (accessed August 8, 2010).

p. 40, par. 3, "Refugee camps were riddled . . . ": Bixler, p. 63.

p. 41, par. 2, "Hundreds and hundreds . . . ": Author interview with David Bol.

p. 43, par. 1, "The trucks stopped at night . . . ": Author interview with David Bol.

p. 43, par. 3, "Dau was thirteen when soldiers . . . " Dau with Sweeney, pp. 46–80.

p. 44, sidebar, "United Nations High Commissioner for Refugees," www.unhcr.org/ pages/49c3646cbc.html (accessed August 2, 2010).

p. 46, par. 1, "Perhaps 20,000 Sudanese boys . . . ": Ibid., pp. 97–98.

p. 46, par. 4, "The environment there was harsh . . . ": "About Kakuma Refugee Camp," *Kakuma News Reflector*, http://kakuma. wordpress. com/about-kakuma-refugee-camp/ (accessed July 29, 2010).

p. 47, par. 1, "Kakuma sheltered roughly 11,000 Lost Boys . . . ": Christiane Berthiaume, "Alone in the World," *Refugee*

Magazine, March 1, 1994, www.unhcr.org/cgi-bin/texis/vtx/ search?page=search&do cid=3b53f1674&query=kakuma (accessed August 2, 2010).

p. 47, par. 6, "The boys were in terrible shape . . . ": Dau with Sweeney, p. 135.

p. 48, sidebar, "School for Refugees," www.oneworld365.org/ news/2010/april/volunteer-abroad-refugee-camp-voluntary-humanitarian-work-abroad-africa (accessed February 8, 2011).

p. 49, par. 2, "Many Lost Boys were reunited . . . ": Ayul Leek Deng, Beny Ngor Chol, and Barbara Youree, *Courageous Journey: Walking the Lost Boys' Path from the Sudan to America* (Far Hills, NJ: New Horizon Press, 2008), pp. 185–186.

p. 49, par. 3, "Even wars outside Africa": Burr and Collins, pp. 284–290.

p. 52, par. 1: "According to author Mark Bixler . . . ": Bixler, pp. 91–92.

p. 53, extract, "It was a joy, it was tears . . . ": Author interview with David Bol.

p. 53, par. 2, "John Bul Dau's excitement . . . ": Dau with Sweeney, p. 163.

Chapter 4

p. 55, par. 1, "We asked people . . . ": Author interview with David Bol.

p. 57, par. 2, "I had only seen city streets . . . ": Dau with Sweeney, p. 188.

p. 58, par. 1, "Clams, lobsters, shrimp ...": Dau with Sweeney, p. 194.

p. 58, par. 5, "Other Lost Boys ended up . . . ": "Migration Journey of the Lost Boys and Girls," National Geographic, 2006, www.nationalgeographic.com/xpeditions/lessons/09/g68/ migrationjourney.pdf (accessed July 14, 2010).

p. 59, par. 1, "Others, such as Santino Majok Chuor . . . ": Leslie Goffe, "Sudan's 'lost boys' in America," *BBC News*, August 31, 2004, http://news.bbc.co.uk/2/hi/africa/3602724.stm (accessed July 15, 2010).

p. 59, par. 4, "[W]e were not told . . . ": Santino Majok Chuor and Megan Mylan, "PBS: Lost Boys of Sudan, P.O.V. Film Series," *The Washington Post*, September 30, 2004, www.washingtonpost.com/wp-dyn/content/discussion/2004/09/28/DI2005040307726.html (accessed August 5, 2010).

p. 60, par. 2, "Lost Boy Isaac Majak . . . ": Daniela Caride, "'Lost Boys of Sudan' Use Education, Employment to Help Those Back Home," *Bay Street Banner*, April 7, 2008, http://news.newamericamedia.org/news/view_article.html?article_id=6280 51a7dc916eac18b1f7a6dcfb55a6 (accessed July 14, 2010).

p. 60, par. 3, "[Many refugees] . . . ": Author interview with Dianna Shandy.

p. 60, par. 5, "Because of this idealization . . . ": Martin Masumbuko Muhindi and Kiganzi Nyakato, "Integration of the Sudanese 'Lost Boys' in Boston, Massachusetts, U.S.A., 2002," http://web.mit.edu/cis/www/migration/pubs/Mahindi.pdf (accessed August 2, 2010).

p. 61, par. 2, "Shortly after the attacks . . . ": Ibid.

p. 61, par. 3, "Conditions in Sudan have changed . . . ": "Draft of the Sudan Interim National Constitution," *Sudan Tribune*, May 5, 2005, www.sudantribune.com/spip.php?article9417 (accessed July 30, 2010).

p. 62, sidebar, "One Lost Boy's Tragic Tale," Lee Hermiston, "Shooting Victim Was Refugee from Sudan," *Iowa City Press-Citizen*, July 31, 2009, http://m. desmoinesregister.com/BETTER/news.jsp?key=499727&p=1 (accessed July 30, 2010).

p. 63, par. 3, "Here are some examples . . . ": Maureen Sieh, "Sudan's Native Sons—the Lost Boys of Sudan—Return Home to Help Build Villages," *The Post-Standard*, March 21, 2010, www. syracuse.com/news/index.ssf/2010/03/sudans_native_sons_ return_home.html (accessed August 8, 2010).

p. 67, par. 2, "You guys should be . . . ": Author interview with David Bol.

GLOSSARY

commandeered—Took control of.

communal—Used or shared by everyone in a group or community.

democracies—Societies that provide ordinary citizens with elective power in government.

Dinka—A group of ethnic people living in southern Sudan.

dysentery—An intestinal disease characterized by inflammation and diarrhea.

guerrillas—People, usually volunteers, who take part in nontraditional methods of warfare.

humanitarian—Dedicated to helping the welfare of others.

Islam—A religion whose supreme deity is Allah and whose founder is Muhammad.

malaria—A potentially fatal infectious disease transferred to humans through the bite of a mosquito.

militants—Aggressive people prone to using violence to achieve their goals.

Muslims—Followers of the religion of Islam.

mutineers—People revolting against authority, often through the use of force.

Nuer—A group of ethnic people living in southern Sudan near the Ethiopian border.

persecuted—Harassed and oppressed, generally for racial, political, or religious reasons.

refugees—People who flee one area to seek safety in another area, often during times of war.

whooping cough—A highly contagious disease characterized by a runny nose and ongoing attacks of coughing.

FURTHER INFORMATION

BOOKS

Bol, Aher Arop. *The Lost Boy: The True Story of a Young Boy's Flight from Sudan to South Africa*. Cape Town, South Africa: Kwela Books, 2009.

Deng, Benson, Alephonsion Deng, and Benjamin Ajak. *They Poured Fire on Us from the Sky: The True Story of Three Lost Boys from Sudan*. New York: PublicAffairs, 2005.

Eggers, Dave. *What Is the What: The Autobiography of Valentino Achak Deng*. New York: Vintage Books, 2006.

WEBSITES

Alliance for the Lost Boys of Sudan
The foundation helps with the educational and medical needs of the Lost Boys living in the United States and Africa.

www.allianceforthelostboys.com/index.html

Impact a Village
This organization improves overall living conditions in Southern Sudan through health care, education, and the introduction of technology. Also founded by a Lost Boy, Impact a Village schedules Lost Boys to speak in U.S. classrooms.

www.impactavillage.org

John Dau Foundation
Founded by a Lost Boy, this organization provides health care in southern Sudan by building clinics and training health workers.

www.johndaufoundation.org/

BIBLIOGRAPHY

Bixler, Mark. *The Lost Boys of Sudan: An American Story of the Refugee Experience*. Athens: The University of Georgia Press, 2005.

Burr, J. Millard and Robert O. Collins. *Requiem for the Sudan: War, Drought & Disaster Relief on the Nile*. Boulder, CO: Westview Press, 1995.

Chapin Metz, Helen, ed. *Sudan: A Country Study*. Washington, D.C.: Library of Congress, 1992.

Dau, John Bul with Michael S. Sweeney. *God Grew Tired of Us: A Memoir*. Washington, D.C.: National Geographic, 2007.

Deng, Ayul Leek, Beny Ngor Chol, and Barbara Youree. *Courageous Journey: Walking the Lost Boys' Path from the Sudan to America*. Far Hills, NJ: New Horizon Press, 2008.

Jal, Emmanuel. *War Child: A Child Soldier's Story*. New York: St. Martin's, 2009.

Naidoo, Beverly. *Making It Home: Real-Life Stories from Children Forced to Flee*. New York: Dial Books, 2004.

INDEX

ABOUT THE AUTHOR

Jeff Burlingame is an award-winning author of twenty books. His works have been honored by the New York Public Library, and he has been nominated for several awards, including a prestigious 2011 NAACP Image Award for his biography *Malcolm X: I Believe in the Brotherhood of Man, All Men*. Jeff has been a featured author on A&E's *Biography* TV series, and has taught and lectured at various writing workshops and libraries across the Pacific Northwest. He resides with his family in Tacoma, Washington.